DADDY, BE MY FRIEND

BY

Shawna Woodward

Interior Image Credit: Blueberry Illustrations

All Scripture quotations are taken from the King James Version

WestBow Press books may be ordered through booksellers or by contacting:

WestBow Press
A Division of Thomas Nelson & Zondervan
1663 Liberty Drive
Bloomington, IN 47403
www.westbowpress.com
1 (866) 928-1240

ISBN: 978-1-9736-4881-9 (sc)
ISBN: 978-1-9736-4882-6 (e)

Library of Congress Control Number: 2018914845

Print information available on the last page.

WestBow Press rev. date: 01/03/2019

WESTBOW
PRESS®
A DIVISION OF THOMAS NELSON
& ZONDERVAN

BLUEBERRY ILLUSTRATIONS

Blueberry Illustrations is an online children's book illustrator. The company is made of a group of talented illustrators who are willing to offer their services at an affordable price. Blueberry Illustrations offers 26+ illustration styles to choose from, and unlimited revisions on all their work. These amazing features are rare, and insure the author receives the exact work desired. In addition to Illustrations, Blueberry Illustrations has expanded to include many other services such as: cover design, book layout, self-publishing services, etc.

No more toys or horsey rides,

"Lo, children are an heritage of the Lord and the fruit of the womb is his reward." Psalm 127:3 kjv

No more catches at the slides;

No more bedtime books to share,

Or sleepytime in a rocking chair,

"...For so he [God] giveth his beloved sleep." Psalm 127:2b kjv

But...
I still need kisses on my cheek
At least several times every week,

I still need hugs at each day's end.

Daddy, I still need you as my friend.

"As the Father hath loved me, so have I loved you: continue ye in my love." John 15:9 kjv

No more tummy rubs when I'm sick,

"Like as a father pitieth his children, so the LORD pitieth them that fear him." Psalm 103:13 kjv

Or sticky fingers for you to lick;

No more flips over your head,

Or nighttime crawls into your bed,

"The LORD is thy keeper... the LORD shall preserve thee from all evil..." Psalm 121:5a,7a kjv

But...
I still need times for us to talk,
And maybe even take a walk,

I need your guidance at each new bend.

Daddy, I still want you as my friend.

"Trust in the Lord with all thine heart; and lean not unto thine own understanding.
In all thy ways acknowledge him, and he shall direct thy paths." Proverbs 3:5,6 kjv

No more sitting on your lap,

"Suffer the little children to come unto me, and forbid them not: for of such is the kingdom of God." Mark 10:14 kjv

Or dancing just to hear you clap;

No more pushes at the swing,

Or silly songs for us to sing,

"Make a joyful noise unto the LORD, all ye lands." Psalm 100:1 kjv

But...
I still need to hold your hand,

And see you smile when I take a stand.

My feeble efforts you must commend.

Daddy, you will always be my friend.

"Let the redeemed of the LORD say so, whom he hath redeemed from the hand of the enemy." Psalm 107:2 kjv

DEDICATION

I dedicate this book to my Daddy. He is my inspiration. He has always been my strongest support, the biggest dreamer, and my dearest friend. " I love you, Daddy."

The author resides in the small town of Maynardville, TN, with her parents and eight of her eleven siblings. As the eldest of the children, she has always led a busy life. She has cared for her siblings, kept house, learned to sew, and written over 40 poems. Her deepest devotion is to her Lord and Savior Jesus Christ. She devotes her Sundays to both a toddler Sunday School class and a Junior Church program. Also, she has worked as a custom seamstress, a professional cleaner, and currently holds the position of an electrician at a home-manufacturing facility. This book is her most recent accomplishment, and her first published work.

Printed in the United States
By Bookmasters